HISTORY AS EVIDENCE
THE
VIKINGS

HAZEL MARTELL
Illustrated by David Salariya and Shirley Willis

Warwick Press
New York/Toronto
1986

Contents

Editor: Caroline Royds

The publishers wish to thank the following for supplying photographs for this book: 8 Icelandic Photo and Press Service, Mats Wibe Lund Jr; 14 top Mike S. Duffy/York Archaeological Trust; 14 bottom National Museet, Denmark; 18 ZEFA/Meier; 22 Werner Forman Archive; 23 Sten -M Rosenlund; 24 top Axel Poignant; 24 bottom Historiska Museet, Stockholm; 25 top and bottom Universitetets Oldsaksamling Oslo; 29 Crown Copyright; 30 and 31 top Universitetets Oldsaksamling Oslo; 31 bottom David Collison; 32 Mike S. Duffy/York Archaeological Trust. Picture Research: Jackie S Cookson.

Published 1986 by Warwick Press,
387 Park Avenue South, New York, New York 10016.

First published in Great Britain by
Kingfisher Books Limited.

Copyright © 1986 by Kingfisher Books Limited.

Printed in Italy by Vallardi Industrie Grafiche, Milan.

6 5 4 3 2 1
Library of Congress Catalog Card No. 85-51867

ISBN 0-531-19008-0

Cover design by Denise Gardener
Phototypeset by Southern Positives and Negatives (SPAN)

Introduction

This book is about the Vikings and about the Viking age which lasted from about A.D. 800 to A.D. 1150.

Until the earlier of these dates, the Vikings had been content to live as farmers in their native lands of Norway, Denmark, and Sweden, but in the late 8th century they launched the first of a series of raids on western Europe, which gave them a reputation for violence which has lasted to this day.

Gradually, however, a rather different picture is being painted. Although no one can deny that the Vikings raided monasteries and towns, we now know from archaeological evidence that they also went abroad as settlers. As their own lands became overcrowded, they went overseas looking for other, similar places where they could start farming.

As can be seen on the map below, some of these earliest settlements were in the Orkney and Shetland Islands off the coast of Scotland and these were quickly followed by settlements in the Hebrides, the Isle of Man, and Ireland. More adventurous Vikings from Norway went

on to the Faeroes, Iceland, Greenland and, eventually, North America.

Meanwhile Vikings from Denmark started settling in eastern England from 850 and for almost 100 years from 866 there were Viking kings in York. Others went to France, settling there in such numbers that, by 911, they were given Normandy as a bribe to leave the rest of the country alone. From Sweden the Vikings traveled eastward, making their homes in colonies such as Staraya Ladoga, Novgorod and Kiev, along the great rivers which flowed through western Russia.

The Vikings also traveled even farther afield as merchants, trading with the Lapps in the far North and with the Arabs in Byzantium, Baghdad, and southern Spain.

As well as the archaeological evidence which you can read about in this book, the Vikings also left behind many words from their language which we still use in English today. Some common examples are bread, egg, law, snort, lump, and scrawny. A number of English towns have names formed from Viking words.

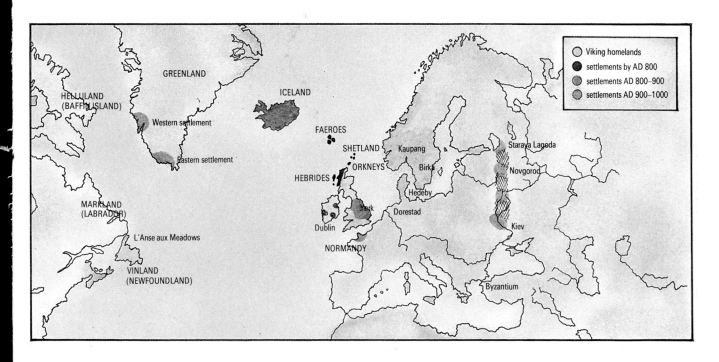

Viking Life

Although we usually think of the Vikings as seafarers, farming was very important to them. So the shortage of good farmland in their own countries was one of the main reasons they traveled and settled overseas from the late 8th century onward.

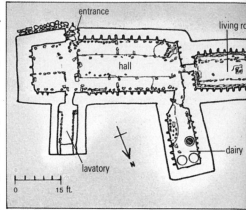

Most of the sites chosen by the early Vikings for their homes in Norway, Denmark, and Sweden were on good farmland, so they continued to be used throughout the Middle Ages, and even to the present day. New buildings were built on the same spot when the old ones fell into disrepair. Because of this continuous use, the excavation of farmsteads in the Viking homelands is quite rare, and much of our information about how the Vikings lived has had to come from their settlements overseas. We have learned a lot, for instance, from the remains of buildings in Iceland and Greenland which were abandoned – in Iceland because of a volcanic eruption; in Greenland because of the worsening climate – and never lived in again.

Wherever it was built, the Viking farmhouse followed very much the same pattern. The main building, the hall, was between 40 and 100 feet long, and oblong in shape. The materials used to build it depended on what was available in the area. Wood, stone and blocks of turf were all used for the walls. The roof was usually thatched with reeds or straw, but sometimes it too was made of turf, from which the grass would continue to grow.

A volcanic eruption around 1104 forced the inhabitants to abandon the farmhouse at Stöng in Iceland, as the surrounding land became covered in ash. The site was cleared in 1939 to reveal the plan shown above and this has been used as the model for the nearby full-scale reconstruction of the house, shown below.

Inside the hall there were two rows of posts which supported the roof, and centrally-placed between these was the fire, which was open on all sides. Directly above the fire, there was a hole in the roof through which the smoke was supposed to escape. This did not always happen, so the hall would often be smoky. It was also quite drafty as holes were cut into the walls for windows and there was no glass for them, though wooden shutters could be pulled across when necessary.

The floor of the hall was usually made of hard-packed earth, though sometimes wooden planks were also used. Broad benches were built into the two long walls and the men sat there for their evening meal, which was eaten from tables carried into the hall for that purpose. The food was served by the women who sat at cross-benches along the shorter wall. The hall's roof posts and door posts were often decorated with elaborate carvings, as were the posts which stood on each side of the seat of the owner of the house. This was the seat closest to the fire. His chief guest would sit opposite him, with the other people next to them in order of importance.

Early farmhouses had just one room in which everyone ate and slept (using the built-in benches for their beds), and did the household chores. Later this was divided up into a separate kitchen, a bedroom for the owner of the house and, perhaps, a room where the women could do their weaving.

The foundations of the farmhouse at Stöng were made of massive stones with the turf walls built up on top of them. The roof was also made of turf and the grass continued to grow there. From the excavations carried out on the site of the original farm, it seems the house belongs to the late Viking period. Three rooms led off the hall. One of these was a living room in which such activities as spinning and weaving probably took place. Its walls, like those of the hall, had paneling on the inside, though this stood free of the walls to prevent damp forming. The second room was a dairy with stone-lined walls and three round impressions in the floor where large vats probably stood. In this room was also a quern for grinding the grain into flour. The third room had a drain at either side and was probably a lavatory. Other buildings on the site were a cow barn and a smithy.

A Viking age farm, such as this one on the shore of a Norwegian fiord, was a very busy place. Almost everything that was needed by the people who lived there had to be either made or grown on the farm itself.

Summer was especially busy as this was when all the preparations were made to ensure that the farmer, his family, his workers and his animals had plenty of food for the following winter. The fields of rye, barley, wheat, and oats which surrounded the farmstead were tended ready for the harvest in the fall. Turnips, carrots, cabbages, peas, and beans were grown in vegetable patches around the house and grass was cut and dried for hay to feed the animals overwinter.

The Vikings fished in the fiord, using hooks, spears and nets. Then they brought the fish back to the farm to be dried on racks, salted or smoked.

Meanwhile the cattle and sheep were taken up into the mountains to graze on rich pastures, and wild animals were hunted for their meat and skins. Wild birds were also snared and eaten. At the end of the summer, some of the cattle, sheep and pigs were killed and their meat preserved for the winter. The cows provided milk for butter, cheese and curds, while the wool from the sheep was spun and woven into cloth.

To do all this work, the farmer and his family were helped by *thralls* (slaves) and, sometimes, by free-born men (*karls*) who did not have land of their own.

Viking Life

As can be seen in the picture opposite, the inside of a Viking house was simply furnished, but somewhat cluttered. There were shelves to store things on and the beams which supported the roof were also useful for hanging things on, such as the two hares and the bunches of herbs. Some utensils were hung on the walls and clothes were kept in chests, but so far there has been no evidence of closets. Food such as cheese, butter, curds, and milk were kept in vats and ladled out when needed.

For meat the Vikings had beef, veal, mutton, and lamb. They also ate pigs, goats, and horses. Fish, caught in the sea and in fresh water, was eaten fresh, dried or salted. Their vegetables included cabbages, peas, and onions, and they also gathered wild fruits, such as plums, sloes, raspberries, and elderberries. Beer was brewed from malted barley and mead was made from honey. Both were drunk from the horns of cattle. Wine was also made from local fruits, though the wealthier Vikings imported it from warmer countries.

The Vikings drank most of their beer and mead during the cold, dark winter months, when they spent days entertaining their friends and relations. Hospitality was very important to them and generosity was a virtue which they greatly admired – partly because they never knew when they might need it themselves. The Havamal, a collection of Viking sayings and advice, says, "When a guest arrives, chilled to the very knees from his journey, he needs fire, food, and dry clothes." The Vikings also gave and expected gifts, which could range in value from a silver arm-ring to a complete ship. Their feasts consisted of more than eating and drinking: poems were recited and, as writing did not come easily to the Vikings, the family stories and sagas (legends) were passed on by word of mouth to each new generation. (This continued until the 13th century in Iceland, when some of them were finally written down by Snorri Sturluson.) There would probably also be some music and singing.

Though they lived in conditions which seem unhygienic to us, the Vikings were quite proud of their appearance. Combs, usually made out of antlers, are very common finds on archaeological sites. Taking a bath was not unknown to them. Indeed, in Iceland, one of them took advantage of a natural hot spring by diverting it into a bathing pool!

Although it is the Viking men that we hear most about, the women played an important part in society. A wife carried the keys to the storage chests in the house and, when her husband was away from home, she was in charge of everything there and could do business on his behalf. She could also own and inherit property and ask for a divorce. Some of the reasons for divorce seem suprisingly trivial, such as a wife's feeling that her husband's shirt showed too much of his bare chest.

Right: The Viking home was a busy and often crowded place. The fire in its raised hearth in the center of the floor not only provided heat and light but was also used for cooking and baking. This was a daily task as the barley bread eaten by the Vikings was unleavened and soon became hard. The flour, which was ground every day, often contained grit crumbled from the rough stones of the hand-querns. This gradually wore down the Vikings' teeth.

Much cooking was done in the large cauldron suspended over the fire, though some meat was roasted on long-handled forks. Smaller amounts of stew and porridge would be cooked in clay pots and soapstone bowls among the embers.

As well as cooking, the women were kept busy spinning wool into yarn to be woven on the upright looms. The resulting cloth was then cut out and made up into clothes for the family. In winter, when little work could be done outdoors, the men would often carve wood to be used as high-seat posts or to decorate their ships.

Viking Life

Our knowledge of the clothes and personal ornaments worn by the Vikings comes from three main sources: archaeological evidence, written descriptions in the sagas, and pictures carved on stones from the Viking Age. Together, these help us to form quite a clear image of what both Viking men and women looked like.

Most of the Vikings lived in cold climates, so beneath the clothes shown opposite the men usually wore under-breeches of wool or linen, while the women wore a chemise, also of wool or linen, and possibly drawers, as well as hose which were kept up with ties. For outdoor wear, both men and women had long cloaks, sometimes with a cowl to cover the head. They also had gloves and mittens of wool or fur. Men's hats are known to have ranged from tight-fitting woolen or leather caps to fur hats, known as "Russian hats." Sometimes a helmet was worn instead, but this was simple and close fitting and, contrary to legend, did not have horns fitted on the sides.

When fragments of textiles are excavated from Viking age sites, they are usually all a dull brown color, and, even after they have been cleaned, this does not change much. But careful analysis in laboratories has now proved that they were originally full of bright colors, obtained from vegetable dyes such as woad, weld, heather and madder. The dyes were used singly or in various combinations to give a full range of colors including blues, greens, yellows, reds, purples, and blacks. As well as making their clothes out of home-produced wool and linen, the Vikings imported luxury materials, such as silks and brocades

Above: Leather shoes from the 10th century found in England at Coppergate in York. Their soles were made in a single flat piece without a heel, which was sewn onto the upper of the shoe. When a sole was worn out, it was pulled off and a new one stitched in its place.

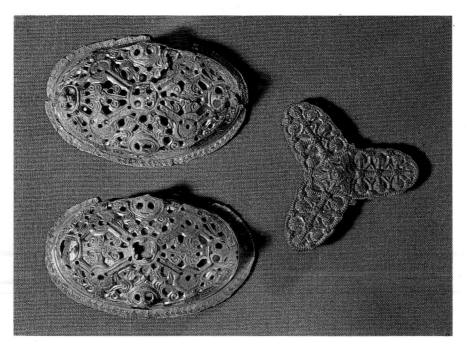

Left: Three brooches which would have been worn by a Viking woman. The two oval ones are made of bronze and are about four inches long. They were hollow inside and, because of their shape, they are sometimes known as tortoise brooches. Between these two brooches would be worn rows of beads, sometimes made of silver, amber, or rock crystal, but more usually of glass of various patterns and colors. The third brooch would be used to fasten a shawl and the design of this was very varied. As well as the three-lobed type shown here, round, oval and oblong brooches have also been found.

Right: A Viking man and woman in everyday clothes. These were designed to be practical rather than fashionable and so they changed little throughout the whole Viking period. The woman's dress reached to the ground and was usually made of pleated linen or fine wool. Her over-garment was held in place by shoulder straps fastened with oval brooches. From a third brooch hung a chain which carried keys, a comb, a knife, or needles in a case. A married woman also wore a white linen headdress. The man wore woolen pants and a long-sleeved shirt made of linen or wool, with a belted tunic over the top. His cloak was fastened with a brooch on his right shoulder, leaving his arm free in case he needed to use his sword.

from the Orient and gold thread embroidery from Byzantium. They decorated their tunics and other clothes with braids which they wove on little tablet looms, often using fine gold and silver threads in their design.

Gold and silver were also used for much of the jewelry worn by the Vikings, though silver – usually obtained from Arabia in the form of coins to be melted down – was the favorite. As well as practical jewelry, such as the brooches shown on the left and the cloak pin worn by the man above, the Vikings also had jewelry for decoration. It showed off their wealth and, in times of need, could be cut up and weighed and used for payment. It included arm-rings, finger-rings, and necklaces, often made of rods of silver twisted together and decorated with flowing animal designs. These animal designs were also used on metal strap-ends and were repeated in carvings on stone and wood.

Viking Life

By our standards, the Vikings were violent men, living in violent times. Indeed the thought of fighting must never have been far from their minds, for one of their sayings was: "Never part with your weapons when out in the fields; you never know when you will need your spear." They had many different kinds of weapons – swords, battle-axes, spears, halberds, throwing axes, and scramasaxes – as well as arrows tipped with metal. They also carried a knife or dagger which could be used as a weapon or as a tool. Such knives have also been found in women's graves.

Of all their weapons, the Vikings liked the sword best. An especially good one or one which was thought to have magic powers was often passed down from father to son for several generations. The sagas – the Viking legends – give us the names of some of these swords, such as Adder, Long, and Leg-biter. The sword which belonged to Sigurd the Volsung is described as follows:

> "By fire were its outer edges forged,
>   By venom drops was it tinged within."

This also partly explains the way the sword was made: its blade consisted of several rods of wrought iron welded together by twisting, then hammered flat, giving it the mottled appearance of a snake's skin. The cutting edges, which were welded onto the core of the sword blade, were made of a better quality iron. The hilts were usually highly decorated, often with bands of silver or gold.

To defend themselves against all kinds of weapons, the Vikings usually carried a shield. The blacksmith would make the iron boss for its center, but the shield itself was made of strips of wood and was soon hacked to pieces in a battle.

Apart from making weapons, the smith was also kept busy making tools for himself and for other Vikings. These included hammers, tongs, files, chisels, and saw-blades, as well as sickles and scythes, metal tips for plowshares, iron cauldrons, frying pans, chains, and fish-hooks. Most Viking homesteads also had a small smithy of their own where simple tools could be made or mended. Archaeological evidence shows that frying pans and cauldrons were often patched in places where they had worn thin, or perhaps burned through as they were suspended from a tripod over a fire.

The iron for all this metalwork was obtained from bog iron ore which was plentiful in Norway, Denmark, and Sweden.

Right: The blacksmith at work, twisting and hammering rods of wrought iron for the blade of a sword. His helper works the bellows to keep the fire at the right temperature.

Viking Life

For most Vikings, their first loyalty was to their family relations. This included not only brothers and sisters, but also uncles and cousins. This sense of loyalty could lead to long feuds between rival families, for if one member of a family was killed, it was up to another member of that family to punish the killer's family. This was usually done by killing him or one of his relations, although occasionally compensation for an injury was asked for – or offered – in the form of lands or goods.

These feuds between Viking families often lasted for several generations, as is recorded in "Egil's Saga," in which a feud begun between Kveldulf and Harald Finehair continues into the time of their grandchildren, with many killings on both sides. Indeed many Vikings must have expected to be caught up in one of these feuds at some time or another as one of their sayings was, "Look carefully round doorways before you walk in; you never know when an enemy might be there."

As the population of the Viking lands increased, so did the number of families living together. They began to form communities, and to follow one natural leader. These leaders were not only brave and adventurous men, they were usually also wealthy landowners (known as *jarls*), generous with gifts to their friends and comrades. After a time, a few of them became more powerful than all the others, and they called themselves kings. One of these was Harald Finehair in Norway in the late 8th century. The kings held their own courts – Harald Finehair's was at Avaldsnes, just off the west coast of Norway, but he spent much of his time visiting other parts of the kingdom to keep

Below: This picture shows Thingvellir, the meeting place for the annual Viking "Althing" in Iceland, as it is today. The landscape, shaped by volcanic activity over the ages, is very dramatic, with a great open plain lying in front of a sheer lava cliff. The Law Speaker stood on a rock immediately in front of the cliff to repeat the Law codes which governed the land, while the rest of the free men of Iceland assembled in front of him to listen. Unlike the Vikings who stayed in Norway, Denmark, and Sweden, those in Iceland never had a king or a royal family, but instead were always governed by "Things."

Above: The Althing met at Thingvellir in midsummer when as many people as possible would be able to go to it. Because of the distances they had to travel, many of the men would be away from their homes for two or three weeks and so they often brought along their families and, if they were involved in any lawsuits, their supporters, too. As well as dealing with the serious business of the lawsuits, the national "things" were a great social occasion. Men wore their finest clothes, and not only was news exchanged here, but also marriages were arranged and goods bought and sold.

himself informed of what was happening among his friends and enemies. Kings demanded tribute in return for favors and set out law codes which tried to solve the problem of feuds by means of lawsuits heard before the local or national "Thing."

The "Thing" was an open-air assembly of free men, called together to discuss problems and settle disputes about such matters as murder, robbery, divorce, and the ownership of land. Each district had its own local "Thing" which could be called together at any time. There were also much bigger national "Things," but as people often had to travel a long way to attend them, they were usually only held in the summer.

Most Vikings had great respect for their laws which were passed down by word of mouth from one generation to the next. The few who would not accept the decisions of the "Things" became outlaws. This meant that not only did they forfeit their lands and belongings, but they also had to flee the country as, once they had been declared outlaws, anyone could kill them.

Viking Life

The early Vikings were pagans who believed in a number of different gods and goddesses, but although much is known about them from legends and sagas, carved stones, and amulets, no place has yet been found which might have been a pagan temple or place of worship.

The Viking gods were believed to live in two families, the Asar and the Vanir, who had once been at war with each other. Most important among the Asar gods were Odin, his wife Frigg, Thor, Baldr (who was Odin's son), and Loki, a troublemaker. The important Vanir gods were Mimir, Niord, his son Frey, and his daughter Freyja.

Chief of all these gods was Odin the All-father, who had sacrificed one of his eyes in exchange for a drink from the Well of Knowledge. Not only was he very wise, he was mysterious and concerned himself with magic and with the dead. He was also the god of kings and warriors because they thought he could give them victory in war. As companions, Odin had two ravens, Hugin and Mugin, which set out each dawn to fly over all the world and came back to him each night to tell him everything that had happened during the day.

Below: A Viking cremation on the banks of the river Volga in 922, as recorded by the Arab ambassador Ibn Fadlan. The ship has been hauled ashore for the funeral and placed on top of a pyre of wood. The body of the dead chieftain has been dressed in an outfit made especially for him, consisting of hose, pants, boots, a coat, a mantle of silk brocade with gold buttons, and a brocade silk hat trimmed with sable. He has then been carried into the tent on the ship and laid on a blanket and cushions. Food and drink has been carried in for him; two horses and two cows have been killed and their meat thrown on board, as have a hen and a cockerel. In the scene below, an old woman, known as the Angel of Death, is leading on board the young slave girl who has

volunteered to be cremated with her master. So that no one will hear her screams as she is sacrificed, the men in the crowd beat their shields with wooden sticks, while two men on board strangle her with a cord and the Angel of Death stabs her with a broad knife. The dead man's nearest kinsman then appears, naked, and ignites a piece of wood. With his face toward the crowd, he walks backward toward the ship and sets fire to the wood underneath it. The rest of the crowd come forward then, each with a burning brand, and throw it onto the pyre, so that the flames rise up and consume everything. Later, the Vikings will build a memorial mound to the man to house the ashes from the cremation, complete with a runic inscription on a piece of wood.

Although Odin was the most important god, he was not the most popular. This honor belonged to Thor, the thunder god, and many Vikings had his name as part of their own, such as Thorfinn, Thorolf and Thora. His symbol was a hammer and many Vikings wore a copy of this as a pendant around their necks. The other important god was Frey, who was the god of fertility, peace, and plenty.

The gods demanded sacrifices and these were made at three major festivals during the year. These were Vetrarblot, in mid-October, Jolablot, in mid-January, and Sigrblot, in April. At all these festivals, the Vikings feasted on horsemeat and drank a great deal of beer, but, in return for the sacrifices, they expected the gods to give them good winters, plentiful harvests, and victories in any battles they fought.

The Vikings believed that when people died they went to a new life in which they would need the things they had used on earth. These, together with food, were placed with the body at Viking funerals. Where the body was cremated, as shown below, these things were also burned. But, fortunately for archaeologists, most Vikings were buried, not burned, and excavations

of the contents of their graves have revealed much about their way of life. The graves have been found singly, in small groups, and in large cemeteries. Some are unmarked, whereas others are covered by a stone cairn or a mound of earth. The ship was very important to the Vikings, even in death, and many graves, such as the ones at Lindholm Høje in Denmark, are surrounded by stones set out in the shape of a ship.

Most spectacular are the real ship burials, where the body and all its grave goods were laid in a ship before burial under a mound or in a pit. The richest of these was the Oseberg ship burial – there is a picture of its excavation on page 25 – near the Oslo Fjord in Norway. The ship dates from around 800 and is thought to have been buried in about 850. As well as the skeletons of an old woman and a young one, thought to be her slave, the Oseberg ship also contained three beds, complete with bedding, four sleds, a beautifully carved four-wheeled cart, tapestries, chests, boxes, kitchen equipment, casks, looms, riding harness, and a dung-fork, and many more things beside which help to build up a very clear picture of Viking life at this time.

Though they were pagan, the Vikings traded with Christians, and they soon began to realize that it could be to their advantage to become Christian too. The sagas tell of merchants accepting Christian baptism while they were in England, although it seems likely that they continued to worship their old gods as well. Missionaries were sent to Denmark and Sweden from England and Germany, but at first they had little effect. Eventually, however, the kings realized, as the traders had done before them, that becoming Christian would be to their advantage when they were dealing with the rulers of the rest of Europe. Harald Bluetooth, the Danish king, became Christian around 960 and set up a rune-stone at Jelling to commemorate his conversion.

In Norway it was more difficult, however. King Hakon the Good, who had become a Christian when he was fostered as a child at King Athelstan's court in England, tried to make his country Christian in the middle of the 9th century, but failed. Then in 995 King Olaf Tryggvason also tried, by threatening to have people killed if they would not accept baptism. But he was not very successful and Norway did not finally become Christian until the reign of Olaf the Holy, from 1014 to 1030.

In Iceland in the year 1000 it was suggested at the Althing that everyone should be baptized. The people split into two equal groups over this and so the decision had to be taken by Thorgeir, the pagan Lawspeaker. Realizing that becoming Christian would be an advantage in trading with other countries, especially Norway, he said that all Icelanders should become Christians officially, but they could continue to worship the old gods, so

Above: Borgund stave-church at Fagusnes at the landward end of the Sogne Fjord in Norway. With walls made of vertical tree-trunks split into two, it dates from the twelfth century. Although it is a Christian church, it has pagan dragon heads as well as crosses on its roof.

long as they were not caught doing so. In Sweden, the last Viking country to become Christian, the pagan gods continued to be worshiped until the 12th century

When the Vikings wanted to write something, they used runes – straight, stick-like letters which could easily be scratched onto a piece of wood with a knife, or carved onto a stone. There were two different versions of these, one Danish and one Swedo-Norwegian. Both were used in either area and were similar in that they were both called *futhark* (after the first six letters of the sequence) and both only had 16 letters altogether.

This made spelling very difficult as there were not enough symbols for all the sounds in the language. For instance, there were no symbols for "e," "o," "d," "g,"and "p," but there were two for "a," depending on its pronunciation. The letter "n" could be left out before a consonant, as in the runes for Jarlabanke's name shown here. This has led to problems in reading some of the runic inscriptions and not all of them are agreed upon. Despite this, they are very useful to archaeologists and historians because they show how far the Vikings traveled. For example, on the balcony of the Hagia Sophia mosque in Istanbul some of the runes of the name "Halfdan" have been deciphered, while a stone lion from Piraeus in Greece, which is now in Venice, has runes carved into its shoulder.

JARLABANKE'S BRIDGE RUNE STONE
Jarlabanke was an important man in Uppland in Sweden who had a group of rune stones erected in his memory. This one is at Täby and commemorates the building of the road it stands beside. The inscription reads, "Jarlabanke put up this stone in his own lifetime, and made this causeway for his soul, and he alone possessed the whole of Täby: may God help his soul." These carved inscriptions were very important to the Vikings, who believed that, "Wealth dies, kinsmen die, a man himself must likewise die; but word-fame never dies, for him who achieves it well." They are also important to archaeologists as many stones still stand today with a record of where Vikings traded or fought.

IARLABAKI

The Vikings Abroad

Traveling by land had always been difficult in the Viking countries, so from the earliest times ships were very important to the people who lived there. It was in the Viking Age that their design was perfected, making it possible for the Vikings to travel long distances, raiding, trading, and eventually settling.

The Vikings designed ships that were light in weight and flexible in construction. This meant that they could be sailed in rough seas without breaking up. It also meant that they could be sailed in water as shallow as a few feet, which is why the Vikings could sail or row up rivers for a great distance inland, and land in places where there were no natural harbors by running the ships up onto the beach without damaging them.

Viking sailors had no maps or navigation charts, so instructions for sailing from one place to another were passed down by word of mouth. In later times they were written down, and some have survived to this day, such as this one for the journey from Norway to Greenland:

Above: A stone cross from Middleton in England, showing a Viking warrior from the 10th century. His weapons include a spear, a sword, an ax, and a knife in the scabbard below his belt. On his head is a conical helmet. This was either made of metal plates riveted together, or was a metal framework with padding.

"From Hernar in Norway (about 30 miles north of Bergen and at the same latitude as Hvarf), set sail due west for Hvarf in Greenland. You are to sail to the north of Shetland in such a way as you can just sight it in clear weather; but to the south of the Faeroes, in such a way that the sea seems to be half way up the mountain slopes; and steer south of Iceland in such a way that you can sight birds and whales from there."

The great journeys all happened at a time when the Vikings' own lands were getting overcrowded and they were searching for

Left: This weather vane from a Swedish church is thought to have come from a Viking ship. It would probably have been set up on the prow where it could be easily seen. To find the correct route, the Vikings relied on seeing landmarks near the coast and, when they were in the open sea, on the sun and the stars. They used a bearing dial to work out the points of the compass in relation to the sun at midday. On cloudy days they could find the position of the sun by using a "sunstone" – a piece of Iceland feldspar which changed color from pink to pale blue if pointed toward the sun.

new territories to settle. By 880, Vikings from Norway had landed in Iceland and were beginning to take their families and animals across the ocean to start a new life there. Then in 982, Eirik the Red, who had been outlawed from Iceland, set out for Greenland where he founded a colony of farms.

Four years later, another Viking, called Bjarni Herjolfsson, also set off from Iceland to Greenland, but he was blown off course in a storm. As he tried to find his way back to Greenland, he sailed along a coastline where he could see low hills covered in trees. Though he did not land there, he had seen North America. Herjolfsson brought the news of his discovery back to Greenland, but, though others listened to his account of his travels, fifteen years passed before anyone else set out to find the new land.

This time it was Eirik the Red's son, Leif, who went, and he landed in several places, including Baffin Island, Labrador and northern Newfoundland, which he named Vinland. A group of Vikings did settle there later, though the only evidence we have of this to date is the site at L'Anse aux Meadows. Here the foundations of Viking houses and a smithy have been discovered, together with some distinctly Viking objects.

Above: The ship burial at Oseberg in Norway, which was excavated in 1904 – the richest ship burial yet discovered.
Below: The Oseberg ship restored.

Shipbuilding was an outdoor job which took place as close to open water as possible. Before the Viking shipbuilder could start work, however, he had to select the timber from which he would build the ship. Most important was the tall, straight tree, usually an oak, from whose trunk the single timber for the keel would be cut. Other trees – again preferably oak – would be chosen for the planking, the ribs, and the cross-beams. Stocks were made to give a firm base on which to build the ship. The keel was cut and laid on these and the two curved stems were fastened on with iron nails. These were then supported by timbers as shown below. Meanwhile, wedge-shaped planks were made by splitting the logs radially (like slicing a cake), and the first pair of these was nailed to the keel. The second pair was added to the first, with tarred animal hair where they overlapped to ensure that they were watertight. When the planks were in place up to the waterline, the ribs were added to support the hull from the inside.

These were followed by the cross-beams and then the massive keelson, which would support the mast and its sail, then the rest of the planking was added. Any decorative work, such as carving, was done then and the figurehead was fitted at the prow. At the stern of the Oseberg ship on the starboard side was the side rudder by which it was steered. Finally the ship was fitted out with oars and anchors, ropes, sails, bailers, gangplanks, and small boats known as "faerings."

The Vikings Abroad

Not all Vikings went overseas for peaceful purposes, however. The raid on Lindisfarne in 793, pictured below, was the start of the attacks on Britain and the continent of Europe which have given the Vikings a reputation for violence right down to the present day. Contrary to what the monks of the time thought, the Vikings did not attack monasteries because they were against Christianity. It was rather because they knew that these sites contained great wealth and were poorly defended.

By 834, however, they had moved on to other targets, as we read in the Annals of St. Bertin's:

"A fleet of Danes came to Frisia and laid waste a part of it. From there they came through Utrecht to the trading place called Dorestad and destroyed everything. They slaughtered some people, took others away, and burned the surrounding region."

There were also raids on Ireland, Scotland, France, and Spain – in fact anywhere the Vikings thought they might find valuable goods and meet little resistance. But gradually the raids took on a different form. From 850, Danish Vikings started staying overwinter in England, and by 878 this led to the Treaty of Wedmore between the Danes and King Alfred of Wessex. In this treaty, part of England northeast of Watling Street, known as the Danelaw, was given to the Danes. In France too, the Vikings

Below: The Viking raid on the island of Lindisfarne off the coast of Northumberland on June 8, 793 was both swift and unexpected. The feelings of shock and horror it caused were summed up in a letter from Alcuin, an English scholar at the court of Charlemagne. He wrote: "... never before has such a terror appeared in Britain as we have now suffered from a pagan race; nor was it thought possible that such an inroad from the sea could be made." Another scholar, Simeon of Durham, wrote, "... they came to the church of Lindisfarne, laid everything waste with grievous plundering, trampled the holy places with polluted feet, dug up the altars, and seized all the treasures of the holy church. They killed some of the brothers; some they took away with them in fetters; many they drove out, naked and loaded with insults; and some they drowned in the sea."

Raiding

Left: The Lindisfarne Stone, which dates from the 9th or 10th centuries, shows seven warriors and is often thought to represent the Viking raid on the monastery there. The Anglo-Saxon Chronicle for 793 talks of "dire portents" appearing over Northumbria which "sorely frightened the people." There were "immense whirlwinds and flashes of lightning, and fiery dragons ... flying in the air" before the Viking raid. This raid and the others which followed it led to the abandonment of monasteries on the coast, such as Whitby, for many years. The surviving monks of Lindisfarne left the island and went to Chester-le-Street, taking with them the relics of St. Cuthbert, their most precious possessions.

The Vikings Abroad

were allowed to settle in Normandy in 911 on condition that there would be no more raids there. Yet in England the threat of raids did not entirely disappear, and many rune stones record the payment in the early 11th century of Danegeld – large sums of money given to the Vikings as a bribe not to attack.

There is evidence that, as well as being ferocious raiders, the Vikings also built up a thriving trade over the years with a number of different and distant peoples. Excavations of the Viking market towns of Kaupang in Norway, Birka in Sweden, and Hedeby in Denmark, have revealed coins and other artefacts from places as far away as Arabia, while distinctly Viking objects have been found at Staraya Ladoga, Novgorod, and Kiev in the U.S.S.R.

These great trade routes to the east were opened up by Swedish Vikings who had crossed the Baltic and the Gulf of Finland to settle as farmers at Staraya Ladoga in the 9th century. The more adventurous among them went traveling down rivers which took them further into Russia. By the 10th century, they had established routes south along the river Dnieper to Byzantium, which they called Miklagaard because of its great size, and east along the Volga to Bulghar and on to the Caspian Sea.

From a colony at Kiev, a group of Vikings set off for Miklagaard. In ten days, they reached the seven Dnieper rapids, to which they gave such names as Ever-Fierce and Gulper. This was the most dangerous part of the journey. Except in June when

Above: Glass vessels from the Rhineland, some of the many luxury goods excavated from over 1,000 graves in the gravefields at Birka on an island in Lake Mälaren in Sweden. Pottery from the Rhineland was also found there, as were silk and coins from Arabia, walrus ivory from the far north, and coins from western Europe.

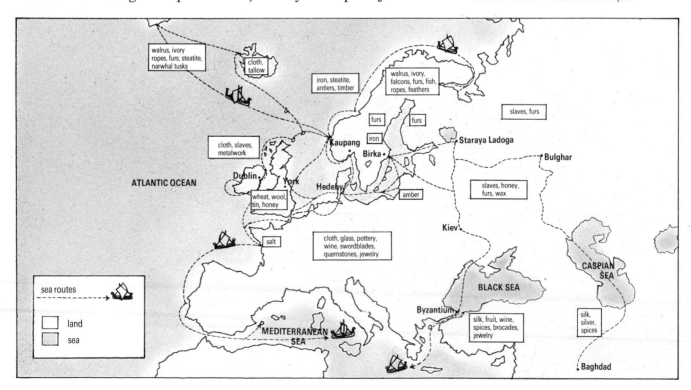

Above: A hoard of silver found in Birka and consisting of coins and personal ornaments. The coins are a useful source of information for archaeologists as, with their dates and countries of origin, they give clues to where and when the Vikings traveled and with whom they traded.

Right: Viking objects, including combs and a rune-stick, which were found at Staraya Ladoga on the river Volkhov and are now in the Hermitage Museum in Leningrad. From the middle of the 9th century, many Vikings crossed the Baltic from Sweden and traded in this area, while others settled there.

Left: Map showing the Viking trade routes and the goods carried on them.

the water from the spring floods was high enough for them to sail through, they had to take the ships out of the water and transport them overland on a series of rollers. Less hazardous was the trip down the Volga to Bulghar, where the king of the Bulghars allowed the Vikings to build wooden huts in which they could live and trade, in exchange for one in ten of the slaves they had taken. From there some of the Viking merchants came home to Sweden with the goods they had bought, while others went on down the Volga to the Caspian Sea, then traveled by camel across the desert to Baghdad. There they found merchants from the East who traded them silks, brocades, and spices, and the silver that the Vikings liked to use in making their jewelry.

While there is archaeological evidence for many of the objects imported by the Vikings, most of the goods they exported left no trace and so we must rely on the sagas and other literary sources to know what they were. Apart from slaves, often taken from the coast of Ireland and from the area to the east of the Baltic, the Vikings exported dried fish, timber, and honey. In the north they trapped animals for furs such as sable, fox, squirrel, and beaver. They also caught walruses whose tusks could be used as a substitute for elephant ivory and whose skin was cut in a long spiral from shoulder to tail to make strong ropes. Also, in the north, whales were hunted for food and oil, and down and feathers were collected to fill bed-quilts and bolsters.

Yet despite all this, the pirate spirit remained strong in some Vikings and not every merchant reached his destination with his full cargo.

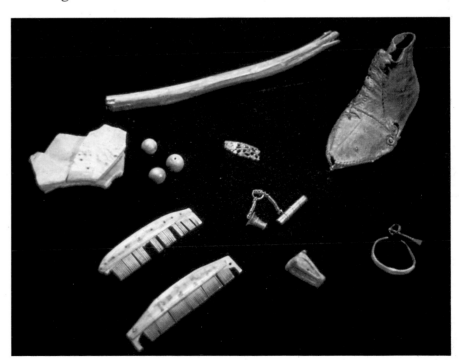

The Vikings Abroad

Until recently, the evidence for Viking settlement in the Danelaw and Northumbria in England came from place-names with a distinct Scandinavian sound, such as Grimsby and Whitby, Ravensthorpe and Kettlethorpe. This was supported by more concrete evidence, such as memorial stones carved in the Viking style (like that of the Viking warrior on page 24), and well-scattered finds, such as a Viking burial in the churchyard at Wensley and a Viking sword found in a stream at Gilling, both in Yorkshire. At Ribblehead, also in Yorkshire, the excavation of a Viking-age farm has helped to build up our picture of the Viking settler as a farmer.

The Anglo-Saxon Chronicle for the first half of the 10th century speaks of Viking kings ruling in York. In 919, it says, "King Ragnald won York," and in 948, "King Eadred ravaged all Northumbria, because they had taken Eric for their king." This evidence is supported by Irish history – Ragnald was a Viking who had originally settled in Ireland – and by Norwegian history, for Eric (Bloodax) was the son of Harald Finehair and had ruled in Norway for a short time. Yet in spite of this, little was known of life in York at this time, as the town had long been built over. Chance finds had been made, especially in the area between the rivers Foss and Ouse, then, in 1972, a small excavation in The Pavement revealed some well-preserved Viking finds, mostly from a leatherworker's shop. Later, in 1976, the opportunity came to excavate the nearby Coppergate site.

Left: The site at Coppergate, York, which was excavated by the York Archaeological Trust from 1976 to 1981. Situated between the rivers Foss and Ouse, this waterlogged site had preserved many thousands of items which allowed the archaeologists to build up a detailed picture of life in Viking Jorvik. These finds range in size from the upright timbers which formed the walls of Viking houses (and were in places still standing more than 3 feet high), to small fishbones and tiny seeds, which revealed much about the Vikings' diet. Behind the houses was evidence of the workshops in which Viking carpenters, jewelers and moneyers earned their livings producing goods for the thriving community and for the traders and other visitors who came to the town.

The excavation at Coppergate has helped to build up a clear picture of what life was like in the Viking age town of Jorvik. By our standards, it was dirty and cramped, with timber or wattle houses crowded close together. Hens and geese roamed the streets and backyards picking food from the refuse left to rot there, and pigs were kept in small enclosures attached to the houses. At the back of the houses, wells and cesspits were often dug side by side. Eggs have survived in the cesspits which show that the Vikings were infested by gut worms, and eggs found on combs show that they had head-lice.

Yet, in spite of this, Viking age Jorvik was a prosperous place. Jewelers worked in Coppergate, producing rings and brooches from amber, silver, gold, bronze, copper, and lead. Woodworkers turned bowls and dishes. Food was plentiful and varied, with fruit, nuts, and vegetables, as well as meat, poultry, fish, and game. Luxury goods, such as silk and wine, arrived at the busy wharf, while woolen cloth and wheat were exported. The number of different coins found on the site shows how far the traders traveled (a counterfeit Arabian coin was even found in a lavatory – presumably thrown there in disgust!). The many different coins minted in Jorvik itself are evidence of the troubled political times the Vikings lived in, for every time there was a new king, new coinage had to be struck.

Above: Children in Coppergate playing *Hnefatafl*, a board game rather like checkers which was known throughout the Viking world. Several of the gaming pieces were found in the excavation at Coppergate. In their leisure time, the Vikings in Jorvik enjoyed music too, as a set of wooden panpipes was found. We also know that they skated in the winter, for several ice skates made of bone have been discovered. Though most of the Viking settlers seem to have stayed together in the same area of the town, they would have had little difficulty in talking to the native population of York as Old Norse and the English which was spoken at that time were very similar. Some Vikings brought their families over with them, while others married local women. Ties between York and Dublin remained close throughout the Viking period and at times both places were ruled by the same king.

The Vikings Abroad

The Central Settlement of the trading town of Hedeby, shown below, started to be built alongside the Hedeby Stream in the late eighth century. On the shores of Haddeby Noor, an inlet off the Schlei fjord, it gave sheltered and easy access to the trading routes of the Baltic, while inland it connected to the Haervej, an important north-south land route. On the landward side, the town was protected by a semicircular rampart which had a spur connecting it to the Danevirke, a system of earthworks which defended the base of the Jutland peninsula and gave access to the North Sea coast.

The Town of Hedeby

In this ideal position, Hedeby soon flourished. The stream bed was diverted and planked as the streets spread parallel and at right angles to it. Both merchants and craftsmen lived in the wooden houses of the town and there was much trading in luxury goods such as jewelry and furs.

By the end of the 10th century Hedeby began to decline. It was burned by the Norwegian, Harald the Hard-Ruler, then raided by the Slavs, and by the early 11th century it had been abandoned, to be replaced by Schleswig on the north bank of the Schlei.

Glossary

THE ANGLO-SAXON CHRONICLE: a written record of events in England which was started in the 9th century and continued for almost a hundred years after the Battle of Hastings. The events were written up by monks in different monasteries throughout the country and several of their manuscripts exist to this day.

L'ANSE AUX MEADOWS: the only settlement in North America which has so far been proved to be Viking.

DANEGELD: money demanded by the Vikings from the kings of England and other countries as a bribe to leave them and their lands in peace.

DANELAW: the land to the north and east of Watling Street which was given to the Vikings by King Alfred after the Treaty of Wedmore. It was ruled by Viking law, not English, and, as well as having farms and villages, it had five main towns, Derby, Leicester, Lincoln, Nottingham, and Stamford, which were known as the Five Boroughs.

FUTHARK: the Viking equivalent of our alphabet. The name is taken from the first six runes which are F, U, Th, A, R and K.

HALBERD: a weapon which combined a spear and a battle-ax on a stout pole 5 to 6 feet long.

HELLULAND: Leif Eiriksson's name for the south of Baffin Island. It means "Flat Stone Land."

JARL: a wealthy Viking landowner who was also a chieftain.

JORVIK: the Viking name for York.

KARL: a freeborn man from any walk of life. Some were rich and others were very poor. They included farmers, traders, and craftsmen and they would work for each other as well as for the jarls.

MONEYER: a tradesman who earned his living by making coins for the local ruler. The design for each coin was engraved on a metal die and tried out on a strip of lead before being stamped onto silver coins. The moneyer did not always get his design right the first time, however, as was shown by a strip of lead excavated at Coppergate, where one side of the coin had been designed with the inscription back to front.

QUERN: a handmill, made of two stones resting one on top of the other, used for grinding corn and other grains.

SAGA: story which the Vikings learned by heart and passed on from one generation to another. Many sagas were eventually written down in the 13th century by an Icelander, Snorri Sturluson.

SCRAMASAX: a large, single-edged knife which was used as a weapon.

SOAPSTONE: a soft stone found in Norway which was easily worked into bowls and cups. It got its name because it feels smooth like soap.

THRALL: the Viking name for slave. Slave trading was important to the Vikings who captured people from other countries and sold them. In the Viking lands, however, it was possible for a slave to buy his freedom.

TRIBUTE: money or goods paid to a king in return for his favors.

VINLAND: Leif Eiriksson's name for the north coast of Newfoundland. It means "Land of Grapes."

Index

Note: page numbers in *italics* refer to illustrations.